T0374034

Mommy *and* Me

Blue Earth

AuthorHouse™
1663 Liberty Drive
Bloomington, IN 47403
www.authorhouse.com
Phone: 1-800-839-8640

Published by AuthorHouse 11/05/2014

ISBN: 978-1-4969-4942-4 (sc)
ISBN: 978-1-4969-4943-1 (e)

Library of Congress Control Number: 2014919378

Any people depicted in stock imagery provided by Thinkstock are models, and such images are being used for illustrative purposes only. Certain stock imagery © Thinkstock.

This book is printed on acid-free paper.

authorHOUSE®

Contents

Canada Goose and Gosling

Canada geese live throughout most of North America. They are commonly seen in coast, park, and farm field. They are big, noisy and everywhere! Canada geese seem not minding people close to them. This is a big family of Canada geese, parents and babies. Baby geese are called goslings. One, two, three, four, five, six, seven, eight, nine, ten, eleven, twelve, thirteen—Wow! There are total thirteen goslings. Goslings from different families often gather together. Adult geese take turns "babysitting" them. When protective geese are upset or threatened, they yell out "Honker, honker", stand up and flap their wings.

The Canada geese parents look very happy. The mother goose looks at her goslings with love, proud, tender feeling, wish and gossip. In a warm day of May, the pair of Canada geese heads their first outing goslings in swimming. Each of the goslings is their loved one!

"Seaweeds are yummy!" A Canada goose mommy munches on seaweeds, while teaches her goslings how to hunt for food in the water. Canada geese's favorites include seaweeds, grasses and many other plants.

These goslings are a few weeks after hatched. They have gray web feet and short bills with scissor-like edges for eating grasses easily. Fresh and yummy grasses are their favorite. Their mom and dad are protecting them from eagles and weasels by their side.

With loud calls "Honker, honker, honker", a flock of Canada geese fly in the blue sky. "Mommy, wait for me!" the last one shouts. Sometimes they line up in a "1" shape, and sometimes they fly in a "V" shape. Each fall, Canada geese migrate south for the winter. When you see Canada geese fly to the south, the winter is coming!

Great Blue Heron

A little smaller than a crane, adult herons stand over 1 meter in height, and are easily recognized by their long yellow bill, black and white crown. The Canadian Coastal Great Blue Heron is a unique sub-species of herons. It usually does not migrate, because of the mild weather and rich food in the west coast of Canada. Herons have low and deep calls "Quack, quack, quack" like a duck, and occasionally have loud calls "Brawk, brawk". Often a heron feeds alone. Occasionally, the heron mommy at left brings her young at right hunting for food together.

A heron has just caught two fishes at once. Fishes are heron's favorites. Herons prey on fish in shallow waters. Once a fish is targeted, a heron stalks close to the fish and makes a lightning attack with its long bill. Sometimes herons beat wings to gather fishes in shallow waters for an easier hunting. Herons also hunt for mice, crabs, frogs, and other small animals on wetland.

A fluffy baby heron rests in the sunshine. It looks like an "untidy duck". Herons often rest with one leg tucked under their body, and so do geese.

A hungry baby heron stands in the shallow water hunting for fishes. It fails to catch one in many times, but it tries again and again. Finally, it grabs a small eel and swallows the prey.

Herons are big birds with a slim and graceful figure. When herons fly, they flap their long wings up and down slowly. A young heron lands on the shallows with a posture of dancer.

When a young heron hunts alone at the shallows, a goose comes with threaten: "get out of here, don't touch my goslings!" The heron bravely takes on the goose, extends wings going forward and says: "no, I want to stay for fishing!" It seems that the youngster has no fear at all! The goose gives up and turns away.

Canadian Sand-hill Crane

Canadian sand-hill cranes are among the largest birds seen in Canadian Pacific Coast. The cranes migrate to the west coast from the north. They fly thousands miles for richer food. The cranes build nest in estuarine areas and breed their young. A crane family is shown in the picture: the crane mother on the left, crane father on the right and baby crane in the middle. The crane parents protect their baby crane carefully. With long and sharp bills, they attack people who approach to their baby. The sand-hill cranes have very loud call "Gheng", sounds like someone blows a trumpet.

The crane mommy caught a small green worm and passed it to her little crane. Cranes' favorites include crop grain, fruits, seeds, insects, worms, frogs and other amphibians.

A pair of cranes builds a big nest with branches in the shallow water of Fraser River in B.C. of Canada. In the nest, there are two crane eggs which are larger than a Canada goose's egg. The cranes sit on the eggs in turn in most of the time and stand up to touch the eggs gently sometimes. The cranes are waiting for the eggs hatching patiently.

The female crane on the right is taking a rest and hunting for food, while the male crane is sitting on the eggs in the nest. They incubate in turn for a month to hatching.

Osprey and Eaglet

An osprey family nests on a top of pole in the Canadian west coast water. The mother osprey at left, father at right, and baby in between, are sitting in the nest. The baby osprey is called eaglet. The parents of the eaglet take turns hunting fishes and feeding their little eaglet. The female osprey often makes unique "Biuw-biuw-biuw" in long series noisy calls, and the protective male osprey chases geese and other birds to get them away from the nest.

The osprey mommy comes back to the nest with fish. It feeds the eaglet fish meat and eats fish viscera itself. The little hungry eaglet opens its mouth widely and swallows fish meat. After more than ten pieces of fish meat, the little one looks full and stops eating. It stretches wings to practice flying and then sits down to fall into a nap in the sun.

Ospreys have solid beaks, wide wings and strong paws. They are birds of prey. Ospreys spiral over the sky, catch fish from the water and enjoy their catches on the top of a tree. An osprey perches high above the sea, scanning the waters for fish.

The eaglet grows up, stretches its long wings, and flies up to sky. It flies and flies. Someday, it will hunt fish in the water just like its parents for sure.

Bald Eagle and Eaglet

North America's native birds, the bald eagles are the largest birds of prey in Canada. They mainly feed on fish and carrion. The bald eagle is the national symbol of the United States of America. During the salmon back to river spawning season in the fall, bald eagles can be observed perching atop of trees at river banks. They look for salmons and fish carrion. Bald eagles often mate for life, renewing their bonds in spring. Two bald eagles are resting atop of a tree in the winter. The female eagle on the right calls "Eer, eer, eer" gently, while the male on the left opens his wings for mating.

Bald eagle's breeding season is between February and May. This pair of bald eagles has a big nest on atop of tree. The female eagle in the nest looks larger than the male on a branch.

In May, a baby eagle appears from the nest. A baby eagle is called an eaglet. The eaglet at right looks gray --- gray plumage and gray beak. The mommy eagle at left is "babysitting" the eaglet in the nest. They are waiting for food, while the dad eagle hunts for fish, mouse and animal carrion. Sometimes the little eaglet stands up and stretches its wings practicing flying in the nest. Sometimes, the echo of an eagle roar "Haowk" or "Glerk, glerk, glerk" in series can be heard through the seashore and forest.

Who am I? Am I a black eagle? No, I am a young bald eagle. A young bald eagle has dark brown feathers with white spots on the wings and tail. A young bald eagle does not have a white head and a white tail, but its head and tail will turn to white in four to five years since born.

A bald eagle is feeding on a carrion fish on seashore.

Mallard Duck and Duckling

Here is a mallard duck's big family. The duck mommy at right has brown-speckled plumages; the duck dad behind her has a glossy green head, and duck babies at left have brown yellow fluffy feathers. Baby ducks are called ducklings. Do you know how many ducklings are there? Let us count: 1, 2, 3, 4, 5, 6, 7, 8, 9, 10. Wow! There are total 10 ducklings!

"Follow me!" The mallard mother tells her little ones. She walks ahead and followed by her little ducklings. They communicate with a sound like "Quack, quack, quack" and "Chick, chick, chick" while walking on the grass. Little ducklings are able to swim and walk soon after they are hatched.

A mallard hen laid an egg in a ground nest nearby the water. The white-greened egg looks a little bigger than a chicken hen's egg, and will be incubated for about one month to hatching.

A flock of mallard ducklings rests on a river bank in the sunshine. With downy feathers, flat and wide bills, how cute these ducklings look! When they are threatened by rats, otters, coyotes and other animals, the ducklings will jump into the water and escape away.

A mallard duck family swims in a sunny spring day. Little ducklings munch on insects, worms and other small animals in the water. They need lots of protein to grow up and have feathers for flying before the autumn.

Two male ducks feed in shallow water. The duck at right grabs a small crab, and the other one tips up its tail and feeds on underwater plants.

Chicken and Chick

Chickens are a most popular domesticated fowl. They are well seen in farms. Male chickens are called roosters. They give a loud "morning crow" every day. Female chickens are called hens. They call "cluck, cluck ta" loudly after laying an egg. Baby chickens are hatched from eggs, and are called chicks. Two little chicks stick to their mommy together. The chick with a crest in the picture is a little rooster and the other one behind the little rooster is a little hen.

Chickens are omnivores. They often scratch soil to search for foods. A chicken mommy takes her babies to search for crops, seeds, worms and insects.

A rooster has a more colorful looking than a hen. The rooster in the picture has a red crest, bright reddish-brown feathers and a long tail. The rooster crows loudly and stands by their hencoop.

Raccoon and Kits

This is a raccoon family, a raccoon mother at right and her three babies at left. Baby raccoons are called kits. They travel down from mountains to look for food in a yard. A kit at left stands on its hind legs to see and smell its surroundings. A little bigger than a cat, raccoons are medium -sized mammals. They are native animals and live throughout most of North America. All raccoons have the same basic colors: a black white face, a gray body with fluffy fur, and a black gray striped tail. Raccoons look shy and try to avoid contact with people. Their lairs are made of branch and dry grass on ground in wooded areas or bush-land.

"There are yummy berries on that tree, follow me!" The raccoon mom says to its kits. The mother goes toward the tree and followed by her little kits. Raccoons are omnivorous and eat almost anything available, from berries and nuts to insects, fishes, crabs and other small animals. You have probably seen them in parks or yards, and they perhaps appreciate the fruits or berries there.

"Bow wow!" a dog in the next yard barks at the raccoons. "It's a dog!" The mother warns its kits of danger. The little raccoons are scared and hide behind a tree following their mom. They keep quiet until the dog stops barking, and climb to a tree to get berries. Sometimes a raccoon mom seizes its baby by the scruff of the neck to take the baby up to a tree when the little kit is scared to climb.

After a meal, the naughty raccoon kits wrestle with each other, cuddle, babble, scream, ounce on their mother and play in the middle of yard.

Squirrel

Squirrels are well seen small animals in North America. They have long tails and sharp teeth. "Hi, I'm a baby squirrel! It is my first time outing." In a beautiful sunny day of fall, a squirrel mom and her baby venture outside. The baby pokes its head and plays with mother on the ground. The little squirrel is tiny and has sparkling eyes, while the mother squirrel has long bushy fur tail. When a baby squirrel is too small to walk, the mother takes her baby by the scruff of the neck feeding outside.

Tree Squirrel

Squirrels are excellent tree climbers and often come to the ground for food as well. Tree Squirrels, Black Squirrels and Red Squirrels are often seen in the west coast of Canada. A tree squirrel enjoys a walnut. It takes the outer shell away and eats the kernel of the walnut. Squirrels' favorites include nuts, acorns, berries, flowers, grains and mushrooms.

Black Squirrel

A black squirrel finds a fruit. "Yummy, yummy", it holds the fruit with its hands and enjoys the meal very much. Squirrels bury and store foods for the winter.

Red Squirrel

A red squirrel digs out a buried apple, takes it to a branch of a tree quickly, and munches at the apple.

Northern Flicker

Northern flickers are woodpeckers living in North America. They look bigger than a pigeon. In autumn, ripe berries are everywhere. Flickers like red berries as well. A male flicker gives loud calls of "Jar" or "Gwreack , gwreack, gwreack" and eats berries happily.

Young flickers need to practice flying and standing on a tree to peck holes and find food. A young flicker at bottom stands, walks up and down the pole, and hunts insects and worms from cavities following its parents.

With a long tail and solid bill, the little female flicker hunts for worms, insects on the grassland. It also laps up ants with its long tongue from an ants nest.

A male flicker with a red jaw at left is feeding his young baby worms. The little flicker on the right hangs on and waits for food. Northern flickers like ants and insects and take food on ground more often than other woodpeckers.

Pileated Woodpecker

Pileated woodpeckers are the biggest wood peckers in North America. They look a little larger than a crow. The woodpeckers have glowing red crest on heads, long necks, solid bills and large paws. They have "Guar, guar, guar" loud calls. A male woodpecker drums on a tree with bill, making a loud "ding, ding, ding" noise, and hunts for insects and worms.

In spring, a pileated woodpecker baby, smaller than a sparrow, is learning hunting for insects with its mom. It stands on the tree, pecks lightly and searches for food. Sometimes, it fails to stand firm and falls down, but it keeps trying again and again. It works hard until mommy's calling back. The baby woodpecker with a red ponytail-like crest looks having her first outing from the nest.

In summer, the baby woodpecker grows up and has its crest in bright red. It searches around the grasses for worms and insects.

Tree Swallow

The man-made nests on a pole in the water are tree swallows' homes. Parents of swallows are rushing near their nests. They give noisy calls "Jie, jie, jie" and feed their babies. The blue swallow on a box is a male. In a box at his left side is a female and a baby swallow is standing on the box.

Tree swallows look a little smaller than a sparrow. A young swallow is resting near the water. It has bright eyes, glossy blue-green head, gray wings and white chest. So cute!

A wood box is the home of a tree swallow family. A mother swallow is feeding her baby insects. By their sickle-shaped strong wings, swallows can fly very fast. They chase and catch insects in the air.

When the mother swallow is away, a baby swallow pops its head out. "Wow, it is so bright." The little one looks at the amazing world!

Steller's Jay

A little smaller than a crow, Steller's jays are commonly seen in the west coast of Canada. The energetic jay is the provincial bird of British Columbia. The bird is characterized by a beautiful blue plumage, long-crested head, and loud "Jay-jay-jay" calls. Steller's jays are a curious bird, and often get close to people for food. Sometimes, they grab food at open tables or campsites. Two Steller's jays are in a back yard.

A baby Steller's jay follows its parents to a back yard. It jumps up and down the ground looking for food. Its favorite foods include insects, worms, seeds and crops.

Seagull

Seagulls are commonly seen at seashore and in urban areas close to waters. They have white plumages, grey wings, pink webbed feet and yellow bills. Seagulls eat a wide range of foods from fishes, shellfishes, insects, moths and bird eggs to berries and crops. Seagulls make noisy calls like "Gher, gher, gher" and grab food from each other or the food left by people. Two seagulls are searching for clams in the shallows.

A baby seagull walks on the grass. It has delicate legs, brown and white plumages. Little seagulls are able to fly and search food soon after born.

A flock of young seagulls catch fishes in shallow waters. Seagulls feed on a wide range of sea foods, including fishes, clams, worms, crabs and starfishes.

The seagull at right swallows a whole starfish!

Bufflehead Duck

Bufflehead ducks are a smallest diving duck seen in Canada. In winter, bufflehead ducks come from northern area to the west coast of Canada for feeding. The ducks dive into deeper water to look for foods, and present in pairs or smaller groups. A pair of bufflehead ducks swims and rests on the ice water, the male is at right and the female is at left.

Adult female bufflehead ducks are grey with a white patch under the eyes. This female bufflehead duck swims in the cold sea and frequently dives for food.

Adult males are black and white, have glossy green and purple heads with a white patch. Bufflehead ducks swim fast and dive frequently, they are fishing experts. A male bufflehead duck swims in the winter sea.

A small baby duck swims in the cold water alone. It has fluffy feathers, waterproof plumages, and a white patch under its eyes.

Paddling its big web-feet and wings, the brave baby bufflehead dives in ice-water, searches for insects, fishes, shrimps, crabs and sea plants.

Common Goldeneye

A little bigger than a bufflehead duck, the common goldeneyes are small diving ducks. They build nest in tree-holes in northern areas and migrate to the west coast of Canada in winter. Like their name, goldeneye ducks have golden colored eyes and beautiful plumages. A pair of goldeneye ducks swims and rests on the cold water, the male is at right and the female is at left.

Following their parents, young goldeneye ducks migrate to the west coast of Canada in winter. To take advantage of the abundant food in the water, a baby duck enjoys diving, feeding and resting on the ice-water.

Opening its eyes wide, a goldeneye duck is diving in the water for foods.

Goldeneye ducks are swimming, diving and fishing experts. A goldeneye duck catches a crab. It holds the crab for a while and then swallows it.

Common Merganser

Common mergansers are large fishing ducks. They are carnivorous, do not eat any plants. Their long and narrow saw-bills are well adopted to catch fishes. Often they appear in pairs or family groups. The male duck at left has dark green head, red bill and black white plumages and the female with a catch at right has brown head and grey plumages.

A merganser mommy leads her babies swimming and feeding in the waters. An impressive feature of a female duck is a longer feathers hair at head. Brown baby ducks have white spots on their plumages. They feed on insects and worms while swimming.

A merganser duck has a long, saw-like bill which is powerful to grab fishes in the water.

The male merganser duck swallows a big fish. Mergansers immerse their eyes in water looking for fishes and dive into the water to catch fishes. These ducks usually swallow small fishes when they are diving.

Harbor Seal and Pup

There are many harbor seals in the seashore at the west coast of Canada. They like fishes and cuttlefishes in the waters. With a thick fat under the skin, they are able to withstand the cold in the water. When seals are upset or threatened, they howl like a cow to show power and may attack people. A seal family takes a sun bath on logs, big father seal at left, mother seal at right, and the baby seal in the middle. A baby seal is called a pup.

A mother seal at left standing swims and looks after her pup at right.

Seals are excellent swimmer, diver, and fish hunter. They are slow and staggery on land, while they are fast and agile in the water. Two seals are swimming, one is practicing a butterfly swim and the other is performing a backstroke swim. They chase into a flock of fishes, open mouth eating fishes before coming back to the water surface. Seals may look docile and fleshy like a ball, but they may attack swimmers and divers with sharp teeth if disturbed.

Bathing in the sun, a pup is taking a nap near its mommy. With a dog like head, fish like tail and striped fur, the baby seal looks like a little mermaid. When pups are threatened by eagles, coyotes and other animals, they will dive into the water and get away following their mothers.

Printed in the United States
By Bookmasters